PAINTING THE DREAM

PAINTING THE DREAM

THE VISIONARY ART OF NAVAJO PAINTER
DAVID CHETHLAHE PALADIN

PARK STREET PRESS
ROCHESTER, VERMONT

Park Street Press
One Park Street
Rochester, Vermont 05767

LIBRARY OF CONGRESS CATALOGING-IN-PUBLICATION DATA

Paladin, David Chethlahe, 1926–1984.
    Painting the dream : the visionary art of Navajo painter David
Chethlahe Paladin.
        p. cm.
    Includes index.
    ISBN 0-89281-440-3
    1. Paladin, David Chethlahe, 1926–1984. 2. Painters—United
States—Biography. 3. Navajo—Biography. I. Title.
ND237.P18A2 1992
759.13—dc20
    [B]   92-20099
                                                  CIP

Printed and bound in Hong Kong

10 9 8 7 6 5 4 3 2 1

Text design by Randi Jinkins

Park Street Press is a division of Inner Traditions International, Ltd.

Distributed to the book trade in the United States by American International Distribution Corporation (AIDC)

Distributed to the book trade in Canada by Book Center, Inc., Montreal, Quebec

ACKNOWLEDGMENT

David Chethlahe Paladin died on December 19, 1984. After his death, Lynda Paladin, his wife, transcribed many of his lectures, compiling Paladin's own words about his life, art, and philosophy into an informal biography, and cataloguing his art. It is upon that loving work that this volume is based.

Lynda Paladin's intention for this book has been to "share with the world the tremendous depth and breadth of a person's creativity, and what we are capable of when we let ourselves move past accepted limitations." Her commitment to helping David communicate and her own lively intelligence and wisdom have been important throughout the making of this book. The publisher and editors extend to Lynda Paladin their warm respect and appreciation.

Contents

Kiva Painting for the Snake Priest

Cover: *1982, 30 x 36 inches, acrylic and clay on canvas*

"In the kiva paintings, I experience myself painting on the kiva wall while I am painting on the canvas. It is like lucid dreaming; I am controlling the dream. While these paintings relate to the symbol system of traditional kiva paintings, I work creatively with those symbols. I remember the story and tell it in a new way with the familiar language of the kiva symbol system."

Here, the central figure, a Snake Priest, is a composite of the male defender and the female nurturing spirit. The priest's energy is drawn from First Man and First Woman. First Man is shown with a bowl of blue corn meal, and First Woman holds a *tiponi*, or prayer bundle. They stand over a sacred rainbow altar with corn at each side, with germinator moths emanating from it. The sacred serpent is flanked by soul stars.

Emergence of the Female Gods

Page ii: *1984, 42 x 40 inches, acrylic on canvas*

Paladin painted this piece when Goddess energy was beginning to be acknowledged and explored on a deeper level in this society; this was his way of honoring the concept. The "horns" on the spirit beings depicted here represent the consciousness of these unseen energies and our interconnection with them. [LP]

The Sun, Moon, and Standing Clouds

Page vi: *1981, 20 x 16 inches, acrylic, Huichol style*

The sun, moon, and standing clouds inhabited the place where dreams-not-yet-seen were sleeping. For time longer than all times combined they remained quiet, but in their loneliness they decided to move together. In doing so, they caused the first dream-to-be-seen to issue out of the void. That dream became the first god of all beginnings, who gave to the sun a great power to bring forth flowers. To the moon and the standing clouds, he gave the colors that they now wear.

PREFACE

It has been my privilege since David's death in 1984 to share his art on the walls of my home with many people. Seeing it freshly through eyes filled with wonder is always a delight. There seems to be a bit of magic in the paintings that resonates with the viewer's heart, nourishing the deeper levels of the spirit.

David was remarkably prolific throughout his professional career. His art has brought joy to numerous private collectors, and his paintings are represented in government, municipal, corporate, institutional and museum collections in the United States and abroad.

It is exciting to present the story of David's life and his work through this book to those who otherwise might never see the art or hear his remarkable life story. David developed a profound inner wisdom, a natural authority, that began with his relationship to the earth and to a native tradition and gradually expanded beyond his Navajo heritage to other cultures. As he integrated his life experiences and deepened his wisdom, he came to terms with his mixed blood and became a bridge between many cultures and times. May his story inspire those who read it.

I have been extremely fortunate to have met and worked with the people who have made significant contributions to the evolution of this book. They have combined their energies and creativity with their belief in the inherent value of this legacy of beauty. Thanks to Betty Bisbee of Lubbock, Texas, for suggesting this book and initially undertaking to publish it. James Conlon of Albuquerque, New Mexico, facilitated the transition between publishers. Barbara Dubois

1980
16 x 20 inches
Mixed media on masonite

Egyptos

The angel of Elohim stands on the sphere of the Earth
where he/she watches over the land of the pharaohs. It is
here that the doorway to the seven heavens is hidden and
where one must pass through the curtain of stars on one's
journey to the celestial homeland. Activated by the serpent
energy, borne by the sacred scarab, and passing through
the Djed mirror, the traveler will be guided by the angel,
Mhe-ekial, into the place of all beginnings.

of Lincoln, Vermont, edited the manuscript, seamlessly weaving many disparate fragments and awkward sentences into a tapestry of beauty. Without naming them, I extend my gratitude to others who have quietly contributed to this project in special ways. My deep appreciation to Ehud Sperling, publisher, Leslie Colket, editor in chief, and the staff at Inner Traditions International for applying their talents to the process of transforming my dream of publishing David's painted dreams into the shimmering jewel you now hold in your hands. May the spirit and the art of David Chethlahe Paladin touch your heart and fill your soul with beauty.

Lynda Paladin

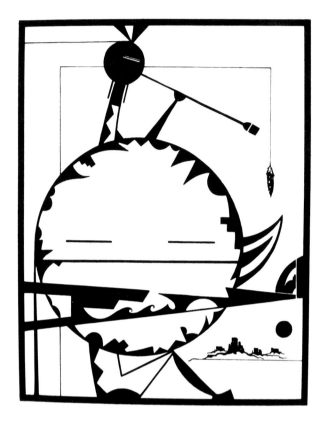

1978
15 x 11 inches
Silkscreen

FLUTE PLAYER

The flute player represents the eternal prayer, the music, the dance of the universe. In the Southwest, we call the male aspect *kokopeli* and the female aspect *kokopeli mana*.

Music is symbolic of a freeing energy, of prayer. As we sing, creation grows; as we pray, the prayer is released to become, to evolve. Each person has a diferent sound, and vibrations continually change; the song is never the same.

Our music must be played and released to be heard; our song must be shared with the universe. Thus the flute player symbolizes our creative prayer, the song of our spirit being released to the universe.

Myths of Becoming

Two of us sat quietly at the foot of a craggy outcropping of rock in Monument Valley, Arizona, as the sunset washed the landscape with color. My companion took my small hand gently, wrapping its soft whiteness in fingers as craggy and red as the rock upon which we sat. He spoke with the slight accent of the Dineh, the Navajo. "Sonny,[1] what you see out there is not real. It is a myth. It only exists in the flower of your mind." As if he were reading my innermost thoughts, he went on. "What you see is a myth because it is becoming, and myths, like truths, cannot stand still. We peoples can only see what is becoming; we cannot see what has gone or what will be. You see, Sonny, 'what is' is only that which is in your mind. Everything else is a myth."

I was born November 4, 1926, at the bottom of Canyon de Chelly (pronounced de Shay) near White House ruins on the Arizona Navajo reservation. My mother was Navajo, my father a Caucasian Roman Catholic priest. Shortly after giving birth to me, my mother left the reservation to become a nursing nun. The reservation, with its clan system, is really like an extended family; though my parents were not there, many others were available to assume parental roles. This was an ideal situation for me to be born into, for it allowed me to be raised as a free soul.

The name I was given was "Chethlahe" (pronounced Chet-lá-hay), which is Navajo for Little-Turtle-Who-Cries-in-the-Night. I was born prematurely, too small for the cradleboard they placed me in. I would disappear from sight as I slid down to the bottom of the cradleboard, and then I would scream until someone pulled me out. I must have reminded my family of a turtle that hides its head in its shell. I have chosen that name as the signature on my art.

The name "Paladin" comes from Paladin Mesa on the reservation. The Navajo are a matriarchy, so children are born into their mother's clan. My clan name, Bitter Water, was not specific enough to satisfy the school authorities, who gave the pupils last names based on the geographical area they were living in, or on a landmark, like a trading post. Since I lived near Paladin Mesa, that became my last name.

On the reservation, my visions were always considered valid. Visions were part of our way of life. Our ritual was a celebration of our interconnectedness with all creation, a song and dance of praise for the unknown god and the healing power within all. We did not fear death because it, too, was only part of becoming. We would feel the presence of our ancestors in the clouds and in the air we breathed. We treasured the knowledge that all of creation is one in a process of becoming. We believed that the most important and sacred thing we could do was make the pathway—the process—one of beauty, always trying to maintain the harmony in our lives.

My earliest memories are of Canyon de Chelly. I remember especially the cave paintings, the pictographs. These paintings fascinated me; they were created by shamans, who used pigments made from ash, minerals, and plant pollen. As children we played out there and left our own marks on the canyon walls.

When I was four or five years old, I was told that I was a sheep herder. I went out into the desert with a herd of sheep, usually by myself. No one told me I couldn't do it or that I was too young to do it, so I did it. I would lie near the cave paintings, studying them and fantasizing about them. That was probably one of the earliest visual influences in my life.

That was always a dream time, living out on the land with the sheep that way, traveling slowly, visiting shrines: places that are sacred to both the Navajo people of the Southwest and their neighbors, the Pueblo. Always having had an imaginative mind, I could almost hear the ancient drums beating and the sound of dancers. I never felt apart from that ancient world. (See Plates 1 and 3.)

Sometimes an uncle herded with me, an old medicine man who told many stories. We would sit around the campfire talking, and he would tell me of the sacred places and talk about the Anasazi, the Ancient Ones, as if they were still there. He talked about the time when the gods came to visit that place as if it were just yesterday. (See Plates 2 and 4.) The whole feeling he generated was very, very important to me. Then gradually it was almost conditioned out of me by my conflict with the dominant white culture, my other half.

During some periods of my childhood I stayed in California with missionaries, who naturally tried to undo my Indian "fantasies" and make me see life the Christian way. I was quite willing to accept their ideas, in the sense that American Indians can accept any other person's vision as being valid. However, they wanted to impose their religion on me and *not* recognize mine. This created a lot of conflict for me.

Between 1932 and 1938, from ages six to twelve, I went to a boarding school off the reservation, the Santa Fe Indian School. During school breaks, I lived with a family on the San Felipe Pueblo in New Mexico and was trained in the Pueblo religious perspectives in the kivas, their ceremonial chambers. When I was with my Navajo relatives I was trained in the Navajo ways, also. This was very important to my life, because from an early age I was shown that truth can be seen from many different perspectives, and that every culture's sacred ways are worthy of respect.

On the reservation, everybody was involved in art of some form or another: my aunts did weaving, my uncles were silversmiths, and I played with art. I was beating out silver and drawing designs when I was about five years old. I learned not to think about what I did but simply to let the designs flow. Now I realize that what I was learning then was how to alter my consciousness and how to move my mind out of the way.

I can never remember not wanting to be an artist. The teachers at the Indian School in Santa Fe wanted me to draw traditional Indian subjects. I rebelled. I didn't want to sketch horses or Indians. I went from drawing pictographs to drawing the wild flowers that I found so beautiful. The teachers thought I was a failure because, in their eyes, Indians did not paint wild flowers. I had a great dream of doing a book of wild flowers; an old German woman gave me a sketch book and I filled it with drawings of flowers. One of the teachers at the Indian School found it and burned it. I had to stand in front of the dining hall, holding a cannonball in my hand, as punishment for drawing wild flowers.

Because I was lighter skinned than most of the other students at the school, the teachers sometimes held me up as an example and expected me to excel in competition with my schoolmates. Once, little Jimmy Yazzi was found putting talcum powder over his dark Navajo skin so that he could be white like "real" people. That was my first awareness of feeling as if there were something wrong with being Indian. The other Indian children resented me because I had lighter skin. I did everything I could to get in trouble, to prove that I wasn't a white man.

For a long time I did not feel comfortable in the white man's world, yet I never felt really Indian, either. But that was ultimately healthy for me, because I had to find my real self. Whatever I did, right or wrong, would not be because I was half-white or half-Indian but because I was me.

Song of the Half-Breed

From Bitter Water[2] I sprang,
And from the seeds of a stranger.
Together they mixed, and in their mixing
My spirit was given breath.

I am a child of my people,
And yet my father's song is there also,
Still mixing with the ancient songs
That came from my mother's breast.

The songs I sing are mixed songs
And my visions are also mixed,
Heard by my mother's clan
And danced for my father's people—
Weaving together the spirits and dreams of both.

I had a cousin named Joe Wilson who was full-blooded Navajo. At the Santa Fe Indian School, the two of us developed a brother relationship that was stronger than most family ties.

Joe was a philosopher. Instead of making fun of me because I was half-breed, he told me, "Hey, it don't make any difference what we are. It's what's inside us that counts!" When I was with Joe I always felt that I was David, regardless of my color. He was my closest friend; he made me feel good about myself.

Joe was the type of individual who wanted to see everything first-hand. When a teacher talked about Chicago, the next day we would be out on the highway hitchhiking to Chicago. We managed to get rides here and there despite being very young. It was the time of the Depression; people were used to picking up strays.

We told stories to explain why we were on the road, and we told stories to get what we needed as young boys on our own. We became very good storytellers!

One time in Chicago we had been eating sardines and doughnuts for a few days and were down to our last sardine can. Joe took the big key off the sardine can and threw it away. I had thought we were going to *eat* those sardines. My heart just went "thump!" Joe said, "Come on!" We went up to a flashy restaurant. Joe walked in and held up the sardine can. He said to the waiter, "Mister, could you open this up for us? We don't have anything to eat for four days 'cause nobody open the can for us. We bring this from the reservation. Nobody gonna open the can for us." The waiter took the can and whispered to somebody at the back of the restaurant. Did we eat well that night!

We used that sardine can about four more times. It was the greatest tool. We weren't asking for food or we would have been run out; they were used to that. We had our own food—but "nobody gonna open the can."

On these escapades, the authorities would eventually discover that we were runaways. They would call the Indian School, which directed them to put us on a bus back to Santa Fe. We never realized that we could get off the bus any time it stopped, so Joe and I always went back to school.

We were punished severely, deprived of food, and made to stand in front of the dining hall with a cannonball in each hand until we fell or passed out from weakness. This form of education lacked something; their efforts to correct our errant behavior were not successful.

One day, when I was still in my early teens, Joe and I hitchhiked all the way to San Francisco. On the docks of the Embarcadero, we spotted a ship with an unguarded gangplank. Joe and I tiptoed up, found a ladder down into the hold, and decided it was a wonderful chance to see if the world was round.

On the ship there was a young German by the name of Ted Keck, a delightful, intense young man. Joe, Ted, and I became a threesome. World War II had already begun by the time we docked in Australia. Ted feared he might be arrested by the Australian Government because of his German nationality, so he disappeared over the side of the ship.

Joe and I jumped ship in Australia, and bummed around Australia and the South Pacific until early 1941. On December 7, 1941, the United States entered World War II in the Pacific with the Japanese attack on Pearl Harbor. Joe and I were picked up in the Admiralty Islands and sent back to Australia to share with the Australian and American authorities what we had seen during our travels. Because I was a runaway and clearly a successful survivor, the authorities thought I would make an ideal member of the OSS, the Office of Strategic Services, precursor to the CIA. Its membership was a strange bunch of rebels who the Government thought could handle certain chores other people couldn't. I was trained to steal airplanes, blow up safes, scale walls—and carry out espionage behind enemy lines.

A few years later, in Dachau, I met Ted Keck again. I was a prisoner; he was an officer. I had been apprehended wearing a German uniform behind German lines and sentenced to death as a spy. Ted Keck spared my life by exchanging my identity tags with those of another prisoner so that I was put on a bus to a work camp rather than going to the death chambers.

Furstenburg Internment Center, Germany. It was a very cold Christmas morning. I was fifteen and a half years old. I will never forget the fear, the starkness of that reality.

Most of the people at Furstenburg were Jewish. On this day of Christ's birth, some seven or eight hundred Jews were beaten around the head and forced to kneel, to praise the God of their captors. This continued for hours in a blinding snowstorm. We knelt and shivered. Many froze on the spot. There must have been fifty people, many of them children, who never again moved from their kneeling position that morning.

My heart was burnt; it seemed to split in two. At that moment I couldn't believe there was a God, a Christ, or anything good in the world.

Night fell. The door opened to allow a small contingent of gaunt, snow-covered Jews to enter. They paused to light candles made of twisted paper and cloth and then began to sing softly, "Stille Nacht, heilige Nacht. Alles schlaft, einsam wacht . . ." The words were German, the accent was Jewish, but the Christmas carol, "Silent Night," was for me, the lone *goyim* in their midst. As the song faded, a young boy about twelve years of age stepped forward and placed beside me a Christmas present, a coat made from scraps of clothing and blankets, sewn together with torn cloth strips and string. On top of it was an American Camel cigarette, slightly dry and yellowed, but a priceless commodity in that time and place; next to it was one match.

I was never to learn where my benefactors had found an American cigarette. The next morning they and many others were herded onto waiting trucks. Their destination was Auschwitz and an unspeakable fate.

Their gift will remain alive in my memory as long as I live. It strengthened my belief in the community of humankind which goes beyond the barriers of race and religion.

I was in a succession of prison camps after Furstenburg, where I saw the best and the worst of what human beings are capable of. One of the things the Nazis liked to do with their prisoners was march them around in circles until they dropped from exhaustion. During one of these episodes a Catholic priest in front of me did just that. Without thinking, I reached out to catch him. The German officer-in-charge immediately grabbed me and accused me of acting like Christ. He then nailed my feet to the floor of the building, driving a nail through each foot. Just as he was about to nail my hands to the wall, another officer appeared and interceded. He stopped this act of cruelty by pulling me off the floor, causing the nail heads to be dragged through the flesh of my feet.

As a result of this injury, I developed gangrene in my feet and was eventually admitted to the prison camp infirmary. The condition continued to worsen as it spread up my legs. An officer visited me frequently who was not part of the regular infirmary staff. He usually appeared when no one else was in attendance. This officer placed maggots on the open sores of my legs; he also forced raw chicken entrails down my throat. I was too weak to fend him off. He seemed to derive enjoyment from going out of his way to inflict this attention on me, and I grew to detest this man and his cruel acts.

When I recovered from the prison camp ordeal, I was given the opportunity to testify at the Nuremberg War Crime Trials in 1945 and 1946. I had kept within my heart a burning hatred from the inhumane treatment I had suffered at the hands of that one officer, who was among the ones now being tried. I was still in fairly bad shape at the time of the trials, relying upon leg braces and crutches to move.

After I had finished testifying to the atrocities I had suffered at the hands of the officer, another man in the courtroom was granted permission to address the court. He said that while he did not intend to defend the officer who was on trial, he felt the court should consider the possibility that the officer had acted to save my life, perhaps even at some peril to his own. The man explained that the maggots the officer had placed on my legs ate the dead flesh, allowing new flesh to grow, and that in my weakened condition one of the few things I could have assimilated and derived nourishment from was raw chicken entrails. The officer had probably saved my life.

The impact of these words was shattering. I broke down in tears as I released the years of bitterness I had harbored toward that officer. I made a silent oath to myself never again to hate or condemn another person.

In my experiences as a German prisoner of war I learned much about the inhumanity of man to man, and also much about love, sharing, and attempts to reach out. It was frightening to see how low we could sink as individuals, but it is wrong to say that the Germans or any one group were particularly cruel. We were all experiencing, in one way or another, something that we needed to experience—our own ability to hate, our own ability to be "inhuman," whether we were Americans or Germans. And yet, in the prison camps I met many people—Catholics, Gypsies, Jews—who each shared a little bit of their truth, their love, their myths with me in order that I might somehow survive.

Today, I am committed to inclusiveness. I believe that it is possible for us to accept and honor the beliefs of others, to sing with joy their songs of praise, to learn from their faith, and to grow with them.

Years later, back on the reservation, my elders told me the same thing. "We're all Dineh. We're all people. In trying to protect our religious beliefs against the sacrilege of the Anglo, the white man, we have become bitter and defensive. We are not sharing with our brothers and sisters. Maybe you can help because you are white, and you are Indian, too."

THE DANCE OF THE MEDICINE MAN

I weighed 62 pounds when I was found in the prison camp at Dachau on a train car loaded with dead bodies. I was in a coma for approximately two and a half years. As I drifted in and out of the coma I wasn't myself. Sometimes I spoke Russian, a language I had never learned, claiming that I was the Russian artist Wassily Kandinsky.[3] Experiences of shifting identity also occurred during the period following my recovery from the coma, and I became very confused and uncertain.

Later, I talked with an uncle on the reservation about the mental confusion I had experienced after the coma. He helped me to put it into perspective and to accept myself. He explained to me that my goals, interests, and ideals had expanded. Perhaps while I was in the coma my mind had somehow been able to connect with other aspects of creation that were interesting to me or that were close to my experience, such as the mind of Kandinsky. It was now up to me to focus upon these new aspects of self and to decide whether and how to use them. I was free to choose my own pathway.

Today, my own philosophy does not allow me to consider the concept of separate souls. Because of my experiences, I have not been able to separate myself from other people. I believe that we share a common spirit or creative force, that there is one soul of which we are all expressions, each as an aspect of the Creator, experiencing creation from our unique perspective.

Yet at that time, still a very young man and newly crippled, I felt confusion and despair. I returned to the reservation, telling my family that I was just visiting before heading for the Veteran's Hospital to lie there for the rest of my life. I also visited my friends on the Pueblos, the family and people who had taken me in as one of their own and taught me their way of life when I was a child.

Upon hearing about my plans to enter a Veteran's Hospital, a clan member told me, "You're not giving up." He and some others gave me hydrotherapy, Indian-style. They tied a rope around my waist, removed my prosthetic appliances, and threw me into the Little Colorado River at high flood stage. I had a choice: stay above the water or drown. I was angry that my own people would treat me this way, but eventually I recognized the wisdom of their actions. They deprived me of any other way of surviving, forcing me to use my body in new ways in order to survive the ordeal they imposed on me. My body would never completely recover from some of the things that had been done to it, but the outcome now depended upon my attitude, my ability to draw from the mists of the universe that which I needed. I realized that I could survive; I did have the power; I did have the strength. I learned that I could succeed at anything by doing the best I could with whatever I had at the moment.[4]

The time was approaching for me to leave the security of my Indian friends and my tribal home. It was time for me to seek my own special place in what seemed to be an alien world.

A beloved uncle sat quietly by the fire, shoulders hunched. Deep furrows etched by the experience of many years appeared as mysterious lines of some ancient script imprinted on the fragile fabric of his face.

In the silence I could almost hear his thoughts forming as he searched out the right words to say. This was to be our final moment of sharing, for he died that night, to be reborn over and over again in the hearts of those he loved.

"Son," he said. "Never forget how to dance. Dance the dance of the medicine man. Call upon the spirit of our ancestors and listen to the music of their wisdom, the drumming of their hearts, and the chanting of their voices. Then dance. Dance to the music of their spirit as it mixes with the sound of your dreams. Dance! Dance, and you will never be alone. I will be with you, dancing in your footsteps, singing with your voice, healing through your hands, loving through your heart."

Painting the Dream

It was in my mind throughout my life that I was an artist. When the war ended in 1946, I bounced around from one art school to another for a while, but I didn't settle down to be a serious artist until the late 1950s. Until then I did a lot of painting, drawing, and experimenting with art. While I was at the Chicago Art Institute in the late 1940s on an Indian scholarship, I met the Russian artist Marc Chagall.[5] I asked him why he painted goats standing on rooftops and floating in the air. He laughed and said, "Because I like goats!"

Chagall had an inner wisdom, peace of mind, and an ability to share simple concepts in a deep way. He was very human and very religiously motivated. As we talked through a translator he unrolled the story of his life and his relationship with the Jewish culture.

Chagall said the Jewish stories were the whole thread of life to him. He pointed out that he also used Christian images, along with anything else he had come across as a youth that had a thread of community and tradition. He felt that all religions were one and that all were part of his own experience.

Chagall drew the richness of his artistic images not from seeing but from dreaming. His images were dream images. To me he said, "You have this beautiful heritage. Tell me some stories." And then, "As an Indian, why don't you just go to sleep and paint what you dream? Paint those beautiful stories!" That meant more to me than anything else in my life. It gave me a direction to explore with my art.

Some years later, I met Mark Tobey,[6] an American artist who, like Chagall, was using dream images, painting from an altered state his concept of the cosmos and the world's legends. People don't always recognize Mark Tobey as a painter of legends because of his calligraphic images, but like Chagall's images they were connected to the ancient scripts and languages.

Tobey and I became close friends. He set up a work place for me in the corner of his studio and I worked with him for a few years. He was one of the first American artists to involve himself in Eastern mysticism. We talked about art as a visual language and as a transformative process that healed both the artist and the viewer. Mark Tobey also encouraged me to take Indian legends as a starting point for my art.

Through Tobey I met Morris Graves,[7] another American whose art and thinking were greatly influenced by Oriental mysticism. He was making earth images using clay in his pigments, and paintings of ghost-like bird figures. There was a sense of going back to the earth in his paintings. Some of his large ones recalled feelings I had experienced in the plaza (dance ground) at San Felipe or the dry river washes on the Navajo reservation. It was Mark Tobey, Morris Graves, and Marc Chagall who headed me in the right direction.

During my travels in the 1950s, I also visited with Picasso.[8] He was very genuine, warm, and loving, full of stories and quite spontaneous. He didn't like having a lot of people around him, but when he did like someone he was quite responsive and open. From Picasso I learned to play—to let go and be spontaneous. The first thing he told me was that I was still "trying" to be an artist. He told me to quit trying and to play: "Here is a canvas, a few buckets of paint. Now let's play!" I learned a lot that way. Now some of my own paintings are just for fun. There is nothing wrong with bringing humor into the arts. A social statement is certainly a very valid purpose of art, but today we need to laugh at ourselves and look at our own folly if we are going to grow.

When I first began to illustrate Native American legends, my images were stilted, tight, and controlled because I thought they had to fit into the stories. Chagall had suggested that I paint the dancing gods the way I felt them, rather than the way others had painted them. "Start with the traditional symbols and then move beyond them. Listen to the story, dream the story—and paint the dream." He was giving validity to an altered state of consciousness by encouraging me to let my imagination flow.

I tried to examine my direction in art. Would the Indian images stay with me? Were the visions, dreams, and symbols real or was I simply playing a game? As I visited my Indian friends around the country, I became interested in American Indian folklore without thinking about tribal boundaries. I visited the cave paintings, went to powwows, listened to the stories of other tribes. I began to saturate myself with stories. I didn't paint or sketch. I simply allowed myself to become filled with stories.

I began to create my own images in the early 1960s, taking the creation stories and myths that I had heard and dreaming about them. I tried not to rely upon the traditional Native American forms but rather to add my own feelings to the images that came.

After meeting Mark Tobey, I began to experiment with texture, mixing clay, sand, and mud. (See Plates 1, 3, 4, 15, and the front cover.) I also did some "traditional-style Indian paintings" because that was what was selling, and I was trying to survive.

The sand paintings evolved slowly. As a child on the reservation, I had loved playing in the sand. I grew up and learned the traditional sand painting that was used in the Navajo healing ceremonies. Then

Morris Graves sparked my imagination as he experimented with earth textures in his paintings.

I tried sprinkling sand on enamel, white glue, and other bonding media. A few other Indian artists were beginning to experiment with sand painting, too. From Tobey and Graves I had learned to recognize the value of craftsmanship and permanency, and I continued to refine the sand painting process and media. Eventually, I developed my own method of painting the design using a combination of white glue, glycerin, and pigment to create a colored medium. I sprinkle clear crystalline sand over the wet medium and shake off the excess sand. The sand reflects the color of the medium. When I can obtain natural-colored sands, I use them. This technique allows me to build up layers of sand, giving the paintings a dimensional quality. (See Plates 12–14.)

I was one of the first to explore new ways of making Indian art, although now, ironically, a critic will sometimes call me a traditionalist rather than place me among those in the new wave of Indian artists, because some of my images are still rooted in my early childhood. I prefer not to limit my creative expression, but rather to move beyond what has already been painted and expressed. I want to explore the concepts behind tradition from different perspectives, developing my own images.

What there was of my formal education I had received at the Indian School of Santa Fe, immediately following the era of Dorothy Dunn.[9] The young Indians there were supplied with tempera paints, crayons, and an occasional stick of charcoal, and urged to create familiar images for the edification of their instructors and a few collectors who became interested in the pictured information about the religious ceremonies, legends, and "quaint" primitive qualities of the Native American.

The birth of an authentic Indian art movement became a painful one. At first it worked to restrain individual creativity, as a specific "traditional" style was developed, and it wasn't long before the market for Indian art became so restrictive as to discourage many young, talented Indians. In this situation, unfortunately, the Indian traders were the ones who dictated both style and medium for many years to come. They promoted an interest in Indian art but also created an image that, had it continued, would have relegated all Indian art indefinitely to the shelves of curio shops and trading posts. Many museums followed suit. In order to qualify as "Indian," the artist molded his production to the preestablished "traditional image."

I might have succumbed to this way of life had I not met Paul Huldermann of the House of Six Directions, a store in Scottsdale, Arizona, that sold Indian objects. Huldermann (now deceased) was quite insistent that there was a place in the world for Indian artists who had a desire to push aside the barriers of traditional conformity while still holding on to their Indian identity. His advice came at a time—the middle and late 1960s—when many young Indian artists faced the same dilemma I did, and I credit him with inspiring many of us to persevere. In his work as director of the newly established Scottsdale National Indian Arts Exhibition, Huldermann gave us the encouragement necessary for the establishment of a new "school" of Indian art, one in which we could and would explore our previously denied creativity. This exhibition created a much-needed showcase for all Indian artists. Those who chose the more traditional concepts were also given a greater opportunity to gain recognition, and Indian art began to take its rightful place on the American scene. A movement which had blossomed and was dying came back to life.

Today, no medium is scorned as the Indian artist experiments with and becomes skilled in lithography, etching, sculpture, and the more conceptual media. Some may decry the new movement as destructive of ancient and sacred tradition, but if art is to become great it must be allowed the freedom to evolve. The Indian artist of today does more than "preserve" his culture. He enhances it with all of his creative ability.

Throughout my travels, whenever I was with native people I would learn their legends and stories. I observed that the symbols changed but the elements remained the same. The raven of the Pacific Northwest becomes the eagle of the Southwest, and the trickster figures of the jackrabbit, beaver, and crow in other areas reappear in the Southwest as the coyote.

My experiences with different tribes have allowed me to build an ecumenical attitude about religion and life. Truth, to me, has become a growing, evolving experience. I have tried to express through my art many of the ideas that I have picked up in my journey through life. The variety of our human belief systems has fascinated me as I have examined and compared them, always trying to determine the balance point in my own mind.

About 1964, I began to flow with the legends. I would sit back, relax, listen to music, and allow the images to form in my mind. A painting would be there. Sometimes parts of several legends blended and floated together. The stories spanned my entire life. They came in bits and pieces: things I had seen on cave walls, feelings I'd had herding sheep, words around a campfire, the rhythm of Indian dances, emotions of love and loneliness. Emotions became a part of my art. That's when I really began to know I was an artist.

I began to paint from the state of mind where images were the strongest. I kept a direct enough focus to paint, but I allowed the images to flow without my conscious direction. In fact, often I was not consciously aware of what I was painting. As in my childhood, I moved my mind out of my way and the images came.

Now I am only aware of the dream.

Shaman's Song

My eyes had been open and staring since the beginning of creation. They had watched intently as the golden sound of eternity changed into slight wisps of dancing, darting colors folding in upon themselves, forming the fabric of the universe. That newly made universe streamed toward my eyes and passed through my mind, where exploding stars and suns threw off particle-like planets that passed from my mind back into my vision.

Dancing figures reflected strange shadows upon cold stone walls. They lunged toward me, into me, through me. Their rattles and drums were silent, but I could see the sound as it formed into minute chips of light, caught up in a sea of boiling, blood-red water and thrown against rocks of molten lava that rose up from earth's surface, tortured and twisted by the labor pains of its own birth.

Those flecks of light flowed back into a vortex of foaming water, drawn into the depths of the primal ocean, where they merged to form darting specks of intelligent matter, each exploring its unique relationship to a newly formed reality.

I flowed with them through eons of change, change that evolved without the passage of time. I flowed with them until the ocean spilled me out upon a golden beach. Serpent-like, eyes still staring, I slid through a swamp of sounds and smells, leaped into the air to be caught by the wind, tumbled across barren landscapes, a wild weed blown by the wind. I exploded, volcanic, pouring my blood over the land. Back in the canyon cave, I flowed once more on the cold stone floor with the dancing

Tarahumara figures, now shadows of light that shook their silent
rattles and beat at silent drums.

I witnessed a world slowed down and almost still, each liquid
moment measured out by the beating of my heart.

Rattles, drums, and soft chanting washed against my ears,
and tears fell from my eyes as I reached out to touch once more
those slight wisps of color that were the first sounds of creation.
Seven days I had floated free of my body, to know the reality of a
billion years of creation, to know that time does not exist without
the shell-like structure we call a body. I had touched eternity
and knew with certainty that I was eternal.

The roots of religion, art, and human creativity spring from shamanic
tradition. The creative response to others and to the universe is the
thread that connects us to the whole. As an artist with strong Native
American roots, I have long been deeply interested in understanding
altered states of consciousness as they relate to the role of the artist-
shaman, even though my own Navajo tribe does not have a shamanic
heritage. My involvement with shamanism is an attempt to reach back
into my own mind, to reexperience the primordial unity.

I have studied shamanic concepts with the Tarahumara and the
Huichol peoples of Mexico and with the Sioux Indians of North
America. With the Tarahumara, in the early 1950s, I was introduced
to my first shamanic vision through native drugs (see the text in ital-
ics above). In that state of altered consciousness I discovered there
were no barriers to reality. This was the same kind of vision my relatives on the reservation had described. During the vision I had become one with everything and experienced myself outside time.

My experiences with the Huichol Indians have also been very
important for my growth. On a visit to Mexico I joined the Huichol
in the Sierra Madre of north-central Mexico on a trek and vision quest.
While I was under the influence of peyote, I went into a deep trance
state. During that time, I expressed a desire to make a painting inspired by my visions. My companions didn't quite understand what

I meant. They thought that I wanted yarn to press onto a board covered with beeswax, which was the usual medium for their art. Instead, I felt something within me urging me to alter my consciousness, get in touch with the spirits, and transfer that experience symbolically with paint onto a flat surface. They supplied me with a board and some inexpensive acrylic paints. I proceeded to create a spirit painting of a Huichol deity and named a young Huichol boy after the deity. The people became very excited at seeing me work with paint rather than yarn, and although my figures were not the traditional Huichol figures, the colors and patterns that emerged seemed to interest them.

During my association with the Huichol I was recognized by them as a shaman, not only because of my ability to work under the influence of peyote in a highly creative manner, but also because I learned to achieve an altered state of consciousness without peyote and to create shamanic paintings that were relevant to them. (See page vi and Plates 18 and 19.)

After returning to the United States, I decided not to pursue experiences with mind-altering drugs. Though hallucinogens may intensify the visions, I find them counterproductive because they interfere with my ability to paint.

I had learned a lot from being with the Huichol and the Tarahumara and from hearing their stories. I began to put little pieces together and to learn what the shamanic perspective meant.

I experienced my third and final major vision in Nevada, at a Sioux Sun Dance.[10] My chest still bears the scars of the line that connected me to the Sun Dance pole. The visions were not accomplished through drugs; we used a sweat-lodge purification ceremony to alter our consciousness. Through the experience of the Sun Dance I recognized that I could alter my consciousness so I did not feel the extreme pain. The actual ceremony was a peaceful, quiet experience. At one time I felt myself tugging against external reality, finally falling into the sun and into the gateway of All.

The Medicine Bag: A Shaman's Memories

Dreams, visions, voyages into the deepest recesses of the mind. The sound of drums, rasps, rattles, and flutes. Endless hours chanting word-like sounds. Rituals, rites of passage, celebrations of becoming. Dancing, heel and toe, toe and heel, until the spirit of the deer invades the emptiness within.

Experiences, vague and worn memories of ceremonial chambers, dusty plazas, and masked dancers. Fasting and feasting, running with head held high and lungs bursting along ancient and sacred trails.

Pilgrimages to sacred sites and shrines. Stories unfolded from the minds of aged and venerated elders. Legends of rainbow people, animal spirits, ogres and monsters, hero twins, and seductive witches.

Fire, water, and Earth Mother. Cloud beings and ghosts with gifts of illness and death. The sun, moon, and stars peopled with dancing gods and treacherous adversaries.

Such things form my earliest memories. Many still remain deep within the folds of the invisible medicine bag that holds the magic used to heal or to unlock the mystical doorway to those evasive worlds that exist beyond ordinary reality.

The Three Worlds of the Shaman

The Middle World

The worlds of the shaman are symbolic of our own consciousness. The middle world is the one we occupy now—a world of density, of dis-integration, of separation. Mother Earth is whole and beautiful, but here we see people as apart from us, not of us, and experience nature "out there." In this world we are victims of disintegrative thought processes.

In a shamanic vision, you begin in the middle world—this reality. You become aware that your separation from other things is an illusion. You begin to see the barriers that exist between you and others as self-created and limiting structures of your own mind.

The Lower World

Shamans can change their focus from the middle world to visit the spirits, the ancestors that linger in the lower world. They are regarded not as people but as concepts. Some of my Pueblo friends call the lower world the *Sipap*.

I believe that the lower world is symbolic of the universal consciousness, the total human experience, the collective unconscious. Every experience lingers in this world, every thought, every horror, every joy. It contains the wisdom of the ages, and also everything we have created that separates us.

We draw constantly from the lower world that is just beneath the surface of our own reality. For the shaman, the lower world is the source of the tools to heal and the tools to harm. (Some shamans believe that their role is to manipulate and harm rather than to heal.)

Shamans confront their problems in the lower world, or the subconscious, and through ritual, dancing, art, music, chanting they transform the demons they have created for themselves in that underworld. Ritual is valuable when it is creative and responsive. When we become a living part of the ritual, the celebration, then it becomes part of the creative process of life.

Artist-shamans participate in this universal process as they create their art. In a ritual of interconnectedness, they create order and balance within their reality through their artistic expression. Approached from this perspective, the work of art is more like a ritual object.

The Upper World

The upper world is the place of dreaming, the Spirit-Talking-Place, the Dreamtime, the garden of origins. It is the final goal of the shaman's vision, to move beyond the human experience to the peak religious experience, which is the opposite of what we know as experience. There is a sense of being whole, of knowing everything. It is total wonderment, nearly impossible to describe.

The nothingness of the true sleep state is the source of all dream concepts. When we reach the point where we are nothing—the void, the source of all creativity—we are empty vessels, and the spirit of God, the creator, the wholeness, can move through us.

Shamanism

The shaman recognizes that two things exist: one soul, and an infinity of experiences and potentials. One spirit fills all empty vessels, all of creation. Each facet of creation experiences and expresses the single soul in myriad ways; thus each one is unique and valid. From the void, the shaman moves back through the lower world to draw to him the experiences that he can use as tools of wisdom to heal the people and the environment.

Shamans are storytellers, sacred politicians, sacred technicians, sacred clowns. (See Plate 16.) Being a shaman is a process of responding to the unknown with a positive "I know." If you don't know, make up a story. Shamans are great storytellers when someone comes to them for an explanation of events in their lives. It is a healing methodology because it removes doubt. Whatever explanation or story a shaman creates about an event is good when it heals.

Shamans create myths to fill the rents in the fabric of creation: "Why did this happen?" Any place where there is a "hole" in the fabric of reality, the shaman can create a story to fill that hole, to supply an explanation to heal the fears. The shaman creates a story that is plausible and acceptable for the moment, always recognizing that the stories change with time as truth continues to grow and evolve.

Absolute beliefs prevent us from responding creatively. Our beliefs should never be so absolute that we can't move beyond them, recreate them, or see them from another perspective.

Science has destroyed some of the old myths, and new truths have replaced the old ones. Yet, to me, the old stories are still true, because they were part of my history. The Navajo legend about First Man and Woman who came together out of the mists of the universe, and other legends that I have heard throughout my life, are part of my "fabric." I will never deny them. I have retained the native traditions and concepts that are valid for my needs today. The numinous sense, the recognition that nothing on Earth is separated from the whole, is valid.

The shaman is a dreamer, a visionary, a mythmaker—a person who goes within the mind to find meaningful ways to respond to the needs of the people. As healer, artist, politician, magician, the shaman becomes whatever is required, drawing upon the creative spirit and responding to life creatively.

Shamans are also warriors, whose wounds become their weapons against fear and loneliness and despair. True warriors are those who take the arrows into themselves. In healing themselves, shamans find strength to reach out and to heal others. They experience their wounds as gifts, as opportunities. Through whatever ritual they experience, whether it is getting rid of everything they have, or manifesting an illness in their lives, or going through a great sadness or confusion, their task is to take that wound and wear it proudly, to bear the scars of life, not as a shield, but as a big open place for everything to come into them.

To be truly brave is to lay down all the weapons and stand naked in the midst of the foe, to hear the foe crying and change those tears to laughter. The shamans know that the wounds are not theirs but the world's, the pains are not theirs but Mother Earth's, the tears are really the purifying rain.

A wounded healer and a wounded warrior are one. We can embrace because we have been pushed away. We can heal because we have been torn apart. We can touch people's minds because we have lost our own. We can speak wisdom because our tongues have been cut off and our voices have been denied. We can run like the wind because our legs have been broken.

The shaman as warrior is you, with your ability not just to heal from what you have experienced but also to know that your experience is every person's experience. This puts you in touch with every man, every woman, every wounded animal, every "bent cloud." Your shaking, your fevers, and your fears put you in touch with the Earth. You don't have to touch the Earth to know that it is shaking, because it is shaking through you.

We know it is time to heal. All of us together, brothers and sisters, are relatives. Now is the time to regain the power: to take more arrows into our hearts so we are stronger, to let the demons trample us so we stand straighter, to let the freezing winds pierce our hearts so we love more, to purify ourselves constantly by being the true warrior.

The warrior-shaman is not the one who throws the spears but the one who rises above his or her own dead body and says, "I have died, too. Now let's dance. We are free. The spirit is ours because we have died. Now we are resurrected from the ashes. Come dance with me, sisters, brothers, relatives. I can never be alone because I have died. My ashes have blown to the wind. My blood has run into the earth. My bones have whitened and flowed into the clouds. I can never be alone again."

The symbol of the shaman is the dying: the going back into the underworld to experience our own wounds, to see our own death; to experience it, to rise as a warrior whose only weapon is love. The wounds we have suffered through life's experiences have all killed us. Each time we take in a breath and hold it, we die. Each time we breathe out, our breath touches the face of all humankind, all animals, all our ancestors, all our relatives. This is the warrior-shaman's vision. We know we have died, and because of that, we are one with everything.

Traditionally, the shaman is an assistant to the tribe. The shaman's duty is to provide the physical and spiritual energies that contribute to the tribe's survival. As the source of inspiration, the shaman challenges the tribe by offering the seeds of change and creative response. The tribe's response to the visions, prophecies, or admonitions depends upon the people's willingness to participate in the rituals of change and growth.

Shamans call upon the spirit of life's experience to fill them with new visions for an emerging society. They empower their people, urging them to join in the creative dance and in celebration of life's truly great potentials. It is said that when you acknowledge you are a shaman all the spirits in the underworld sing with joy, and all the spirits in the upper worlds echo that joy. That joy manifests every time you touch someone in healing. Let it be done in beauty. It is our way. It is the Beauty Way.

Shaman's Poem

Thunder Who Speaks From the Mountain, I am.
Sun Bear, I am.
Turtle Who Cries in the Night, I am.[11]

Three voices speak from my sacred mountain.
I am heard.
Thunder voice speaks, I shudder.
Sun voice speaks, I burn.
Turtle voice speaks, I cry.

All three of my voices speak.
I am thunder, fire, and water,
mixed at the foot of my sacred mountain.

My voices speak,
rising up like eagle wings.
My voices speak,
wrapping life in soft dreams.

GIFT OF THE DANCING GODS

A true artist is more than merely creative. He is a channel through which impressions flow and reemerge, bearing the mark of the spirits that have influenced him. As an Indian, I flavor my work with the spirit of my Navajo upbringing and the other peoples I have encountered. The folklore and legends of the Native Americans serve as my point of departure. I plan not to specifically illustrate a creation story or legend but to capture the spirit behind it: the evolution, the creation, the structure of the universe as experienced by a native people. In that manner I share more than the concepts at an intellectual level; I also share the spiritual concepts with the viewer. I translate my concepts into symbols so people can then take those symbols and retranslate them into their own concepts.

Most of the symbols I use reflect universal spiritual concepts. Some people think that Native Americans are pantheists because they portray sun gods, rain spirits, and so on. That isn't so, at all. We see the wonder of creation in everything, including ourselves, and we recognize the validity of all creation. When we paint a bird spirit, it is symbolic of the spirit of all birds. The *kachina* of the Pueblo Indians that I portray in my paintings are spirit figures representing the creative and natural forces in the universe. (See Plate 8.)

There may be times in our personal evolution when we become aware of archetypal themes that exist within the universal consciousness, and we draw upon them, regardless of their cultural or tribal origin. When we are inspired by that archetypal source, the concepts and symbols have a sense of time-lessness and universality. (See Plates 16–31.)

Art and the Altered State of Consciousness

Western culture has limited itself to a narrow perception of reality, relying only upon the five senses. Experiences other than physical sense perceptions are realities, too. Shamanic tribes perceive reality beyond the normal physical senses. Personal experience with the Navajo, Pueblo, Kiowa, Cheyenne, Sioux, native Mexicans, Northwestern tribes, and Australian aborigines have caused me to recognize that indigenous people experience and manifest their reality differently. We recognize that we are the sum of all humankind's experience. What somebody else might call mysterious or occult is just part of the way we celebrate our connectedness with everything.

When I am painting, my consciousness state is a combination of broad and narrow focus. I make decisions in the narrow focus while daydreaming in the broad focus, the source of my inspiration. I have trained myself to hold a broad focus of consciousness and to work in it for long periods of time. Everyone uses this level of consciousness in seeking a creative solution to a problem. The focus changes from that of the ordinary waking mind; you are "asleep" as you reach out to a broader focus. The ability to draw upon this expanded source of information is unlimited. It is possible to touch anything in that state.

This technique allows me a wide, deep ground of inspiration for my paintings, with the joy of unbridled exploration and a release from the technological limitations of the more traditional approaches to art. I always experience a sense of wonderment upon the completion of art created in an altered state of consciousness, because I am not involved in consciously manipulating the images. There is a sense of total involvement and interconnectedness with all of creation. At times, a brushstroke seems lyrical; a color or texture seems to stimulate total sensory awareness. I flow with the creative spirit, allowing it to affect me at all levels.

When "I" move aside to allow access to a wider awareness, my sense of ego disappears and my identity is strengthened. The ego is the survival tool we use to know where we are, what we are doing, how to react in a threatening situation. It keeps us from harm. But our true identity is beyond the ego, in the universal consciousness, where we can touch ideas or symbols unlimited by boundaries of time or culture.

For example, I have experienced the Huichol people and the symbol system that expresses their mythology. In the early 1980s I recognized that I could allow my consciousness to float into their world view while painting, to retell some of their stories or to tune in to their mythical world construct. Such paintings then have a Huichol sense to them (See page vi and Plates 18 and 19), although I may explore the same concept in a kiva painting, using designs inspired by those I have seen on kiva walls. (See front cover painting.) In both kinds of paintings I am making a personal interpretation using traditional symbols.

I try not to have any preconceptions about the way a painting will look when it is finished. I relax and alter my consciousness, and then things begin to happen spontaneously. Sometimes I choose not to direct my mind to a specific ethnic consciousness (Huichol or American Indian, for example), preferring to go beyond for a new set of symbols. In the state of consciousness that I use in painting, a tremendous variety of images forms in my mind. I am reinterpreting concepts into a symbol system that is not familiar or traditional. I try to tune into the concept as it might exist in the universal consciousness. Perhaps I am reaching back to the origin of a concept. Perhaps what's emerging in my painting is a new language or symbol system, rather than an ancient one.

Though I may start a painting by thinking of an American Indian concept from a creation legend, what manifests on the canvas may sometimes even contain strange calligraphic forms that cannot be identified as Indian at all. (See Plates 27–30.)

With the calligraphic symbol paintings, I go beyond a particular belief system to a reality of abstract thought forms. I erase all the known symbols and start constructing a new alphabet, a new symbol system. My mind is relaxed, with a soft focus, in a daydream mode of consciousness. I am aware of changing, shifting images in my mind.

I don't know why the calligraphic forms appear. Kandinsky's geometric forms give a sense of order, of resonating in certain areas; they are like a language. The calligraphic thought forms are also a language. I think that Kandinsky and I are painting the structure of the universe, tuning into the collective consciousness, each of us telling the stories and seeing the reality in a unique way.

When I am through with the painting, I seem to understand what it has to say. However, I may misinterpret it when I then say something about it because I am taking an abstract concept and explaining it within the limitations of the English language.

The kiva, Huichol, and symbol paintings are like three different languages. The symbol paintings use the most abstract semantic system. When I paint in the Huichol or kiva style, I tune into the consciousness that experiences the world in a certain way. The painting will be in a symbol system familiar to that consciousness. In the symbol paintings, I am trying to move beyond all limitations into a broader area of unfamiliar symbols. There may be recognizable designs in the symbol paintings, such as serpents when I am exploring a Native American reality, or scarabs for an Egyptian concept, but the thought forms and the calligraphy stand on their own. The identifiable symbols are links to this reality. The calligraphy expresses a concept one way, and the familiar symbols add to it.

Sometimes the concepts seem like images out of science fiction or the myths of Atlantis or other ancient cultures. I'm not certain that they are ancient rather than current or future. They seem rather to be universal concepts, dreams, visions. This art is a mysterious language, a new metaphor that may evoke ancient memories within the viewer. It portrays universal myths that never die but constantly change and evolve, so they are ancient and new at the same time. The Atlantis of yesterday may be the world of tomorrow.

The use of these symbols as a new language is a response to my personal need to go beyond limitations. Some people resonate to these paintings without knowing why; they enjoy experiencing the symbols and their responses on an intuitive level. Perhaps those who respond to this style of art also long to move beyond the limitations they have accepted. The symbols help us to step out of the restrictions we have placed upon ourselves.

With free use of color, form, texture, and a variety of experimental media, I express the stuff of my dreams, free of limitations on style, form, or content. I paint because I wish to share with others the joy, mystery, and beauty of life as I perceive it.

When I was a child on the reservation I learned that things are not always what they appear to be. Although I was a human being, I could also be a deer or an ear of corn; I could become one with anything I wanted to experience. When I look back at my life experiences, they are no more real to me than if they were in a storybook. Maybe that is the beauty of it. Life in the past is a story to learn from, and the present is something to experience. It is all changeable, all myth, all celebration, all learning.

I believe that any event from a person's past immediately becomes a myth, a personal story. We can live with a negative myth because we believe we have a duty to prove that the world is not good. This is a valid perspective. However, I feel differently. To me, pain is something that we cannot reexperience. Only in our mind and our imagination can we create a myth out of the pain we have suffered in a heart attack, a prison camp, an accident. We can never really recapture that pain. We can more easily experience the joy, love, and happiness of the past. If we are alive to tell the story, then we have grown beyond the experience.

I sketch in lines sometimes when I paint, but often I paint over them with a different design. I am the dreamer; I am the artist. The dream is mine, and I can change it. The wonderful thing about the psyche, the spirit, is that it, too, is changeable. It does not have to remain static or scarred. There is no such thing as failure or a problem. There are only different ways of succeeding. Every event in our life that appears to be negative pushes us toward success, not away from it.

To me, the experience of living is like having a coin and examining both sides of it to make sure it is a real coin and not a trick two-headed one. To experience both sides of the coin completes the reality for me. An unpleasant experience can be something different when viewed from another perspective. If we want to be chained to an experience, we can be. Some people allow an experience from the past, good or bad, to become the only reality in their present life.

The key word is balance. No Navajo believes that if he walks in beauty he will be eternally surrounded by bliss. The idea is to walk the narrow path between the negative and the positive, keeping yourself centered.

Emphasizing only happiness or only suffering to the exclusion of its opposite is limiting the experience. When you blend the good and the bad you learn to dance and flow with both expressions. There is a greater reality which encompasses individual life experiences. When you take all of your experiences and blend them, you create a new color, a new symbol, a new vibration. The obvious reality has been transformed.

Perhaps there is just one creation and one moment that exists outside time and space. In our lives we are simply slowing it down and experiencing it, each in our different ways. I believe that we are here to reflect the totality of creation, to experience what we already know, to dance the dance of life, and to celebrate it and each other.

Healing is anything that contributes to a sense of harmony and unity. Shamans and medicine persons from many tribes have taken the responsibility for planting seeds of change for an awakening, to help provide the delicate balance needed to heal the wounds that now ravage our personal, spiritual, and collective realities.

For me, art is a magical method of ordering and healing. Creative art and creative life mean removing the self-imposed barriers between reality and what we can express of it. As an artist, I share my inner visions, which speak of harmony, balance, and our interconnectedness with all of life and the universe.

Through my art, I have tried to reflect my personal conviction that creativity stems from the total human experience rather than from a narrow cultural perspective. I have always felt a deep interconnection with humankind's continuing search for truth and wholeness. We must somehow join with the great religions and belief systems of the world in recognizing that no spirit can exist, by any name, unless it is nourished by the openness and vulnerability of unconditional love, a condition of love that motivates us to be actively responsive to the needs of our fellow human beings and to the environment in which we exist.

Somehow we have come to think of responsibility as being a burden. To me, responsibility is the ability to respond, to offer the "privilege of service."

When I was confused and in despair at the end of the war, I wanted to withdraw from life. During my visit to the reservation I found an uncle to talk with. I told him what was on my mind. He said to me, "When the dancing gods created the Earth they gave us one gift: the ability to respond. You know what the one sin is? It is not to respond. When you respond negatively you're still doing the best you can. But always move beyond it. Keep dancing, keep moving, never let that experience, that judgment, hold you back. Always respond to the best of your ability and never condemn yourself for that response. Don't hang onto it; let it go. Dance, dance!"

When I draw upon my creativity, there is no problem that I cannot respond to. Service does not mean giving up more than you can, or giving until it hurts. Just a simple touch and a feeling of being one with people are required to begin to heal a traumatic situation. It is my hope that as human beings we are growing to a point where we can celebrate our differences and recognize the validity of each other's reality. We can heal the world through the simple act of accepting the validity of people who experience the world differently from the way we do.

I have always considered art to be more important than the artist. To experience beauty, one must become part of the harmony that is the Creator's most sacred vision. I believe that art must contribute to the creation of a harmonious environment if it is to be considered true art. The ancient shaman was aware of the effects of color, form, and composition on the physical and psychological nature of people. My art springs from my desire to assist in the healing of the viewer and society. I hope that my paintings awaken in others the knowledge of their own creative potential, and that this awakened potential will be used for the good of all humankind and for the preservation of Mother Earth.

If I have a message to share with others, it is that we should each see ourselves not as merely another person doing another thing, but as magicians, as healers, as lovers of humanity, as givers and sharers. From that perspective, living becomes an art in itself. Then everything we do becomes magic!

I cannot fear death. To me, death is the gateway to sharing even more of my total being with my fellow humans. Through death one is wedded with the totality of life itself. The final prayer of any person should express a willingness to share his or her total being with the divinity that touches the face of all creation.

If I could have a gift other than creativity to give to humankind, it would be the gift of unity in the form of understanding, acceptance, kindness, and love.

David Chethlahe Paladin
1926–1984

THE
PAINTED DREAMS

CANYON SHRINE REFLECTIONS

In the caves of Canyon de Chelly
I would build a campfire near the paintings
and lie there fantasizing that the figures were alive
and dancing and telling stories.

1982
40 x 40 inches
Acrylic and clay
on canvas
Plate 1

Ancient Ones
of the Purple Cave

The mythological gods are portrayed in animal
and human form, honored as sacred ancestors.
Someday, in some distant future, we too will be
honored as the progenitors of all that survives
the advances of time and age.

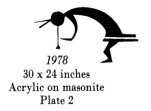

1978
30 x 24 inches
Acrylic on masonite
Plate 2

AND THE CAVE WALL
SPEAKS OF MANY WONDERS

The American Indians of prehistoric times left behind a rich heritage of primitive art on the cave walls and cliffs of the Southwestern United States. These paintings were created by shamans who used pigments made from ash, mineral, and plant pollen.

I am familiar with the style and content of this type of painting because I was raised on the Navajo reservation, which abounds with many fine examples of this primitive art form. I paint from memories gathered as a child, when I spent hours looking at these strange figures from the past. To me, they became a symbol of the rich cultural heritage left by my ancestors. I have never felt apart from that ancient world.

1981
30 x 24 inches
Acrylic, sand, and clay
on masonite
Plate 3

CLEAR CREEK ODYSSEY

Two *koshares* (clowns) flank the perimeter of a huge wind-carved depression near Clear Creek, a site on the part of the Navajo reservation that lies in northeastern Arizona. Although now almost indiscernible, the original cave paintings were thought by the Navajo to be a major shrine of the Anasazi, the Ancient Ones. Its location was kept secret by the Water Clan, who claimed that at the foot of the cave wall was a spring from which they had entered this world from the previous one. The other figures in this painting represent clan symbols, the sun and desert animals, and the maze of life.

1982
42 x 60 inches
Acrylic and clay
on canvas
Plate 4

SUN GOD

My native training taught me to believe that God
was all. The ancestors and all of creation were a part
of everything that we perceived. Everything that had
ever been was us. God was in the food we ate and in
the dish that held the food. God was a numinous
Creator Spirit that bound us all together. It was
our experience of everything in creation that was
the Creator.

1968
18 x 12 inches
Acrylic on masonite
Plate 5

Four Faces of God

I believe that we share a common spirit or creative force, that there is one soul of which we are all expressions, each an aspect of the Creator, experiencing creation from our unique perspective.

1975
48 x 24 inches
Oil on canvas
Plate 6

FATHER SUN, SISTER MOON

In my dream I see it.
Father Sun stands alone upon
The silent soul of the moon.

In my dream I see it.
Sister Moon stands alone upon
The silent soul of the sun.

In my dream I see it.
I am the sun and I am the moon.
Only my eyes tell me it is not so.

In my dream I see it.
I am all that I know,
And all that I know is nothing
But a dream.

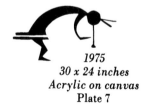

1975
30 x 24 inches
Acrylic on canvas
Plate 7

THREE KACHINAS

The *kachinas* of the Pueblo and Hopi Indians of the Southwest that I portray in my paintings are spirit figures representing the creative and natural forces in the universe. The *kachinas* spring from the depths of our sacred longing, through our dreams, to guide and teach us the secrets of the universe.

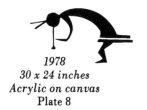

1978
30 x 24 inches
Acrylic on canvas
Plate 8

Seven Houses of the Sacred Sun

Seven houses of the sacred sun
Stand like tall pillars,
Houses of the gods,
Where dreams are woven into souls.

Seven houses of the sacred sun,
Supporting the heavens and the earth,
Where newly woven souls
Dream of man and all else that is.

Seven houses of the sacred sun,
Homes to which all will return
When soul dreams are finished
And gods choose to rest.

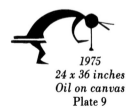

1975
24 x 36 inches
Oil on canvas
Plate 9

BADGER CLAN'S ALTAR

"You have this beautiful heritage," Marc Chagall
said to me. "Just go to sleep and paint what you
dream. Paint those beautiful stories!"

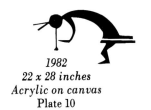

1982
22 x 28 inches
Acrylic on canvas
Plate 10

Altar of the Eagle Clan

The Eagle Spirit, guardian of the heavens, has lent
his name to the Eagle Clan in order that the clan
may hold sacred the ways and customs that were
shared with humankind at the beginning of creation.
The Eagle Priest is the keeper of these ancient
traditions of both Hopi and Pueblo Indians.

1984
20 x 16 inches
Acrylic and construction
on canvas
Plate 11

Eagle Altar

As a child on the reservation, I loved playing in the sand. As I grew up I learned the traditional sand painting that is used in the Navajo healing ceremonies. The Navajo medicine person uses the "sings" (stories) of the ritual to help assess a disorder. He watches the person's body react as the sings are recited.

The paintings used for healing are symbolic of centering the person on the earth, calling in the forces necessary to correct the imbalance. Near the end of the ritual, the painting is destroyed to release the transformational energies summoned for healing.

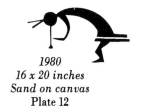

1980
16 x 20 inches
Sand on canvas
Plate 12

Pueblo Mandala

Each bowl is spun from a woman's dream
And blest with soil from the bosom of Mother Earth,
Caressed by the soft hands of its maker,
And fired with the warmth of Sun God's gift.
I take your fragments, crushing them into sand,
And reweave them, mixing in threads of my own
  dream.
Mandala of beauty that was,
Mandala of beauty that is,
Circle of living dreams,
Mix your dreams with the dreams of
Those who behold you.
In beauty complete the circle
That is life itself.

1975
24 x 24 inches
Sand on canvas
Plate 13

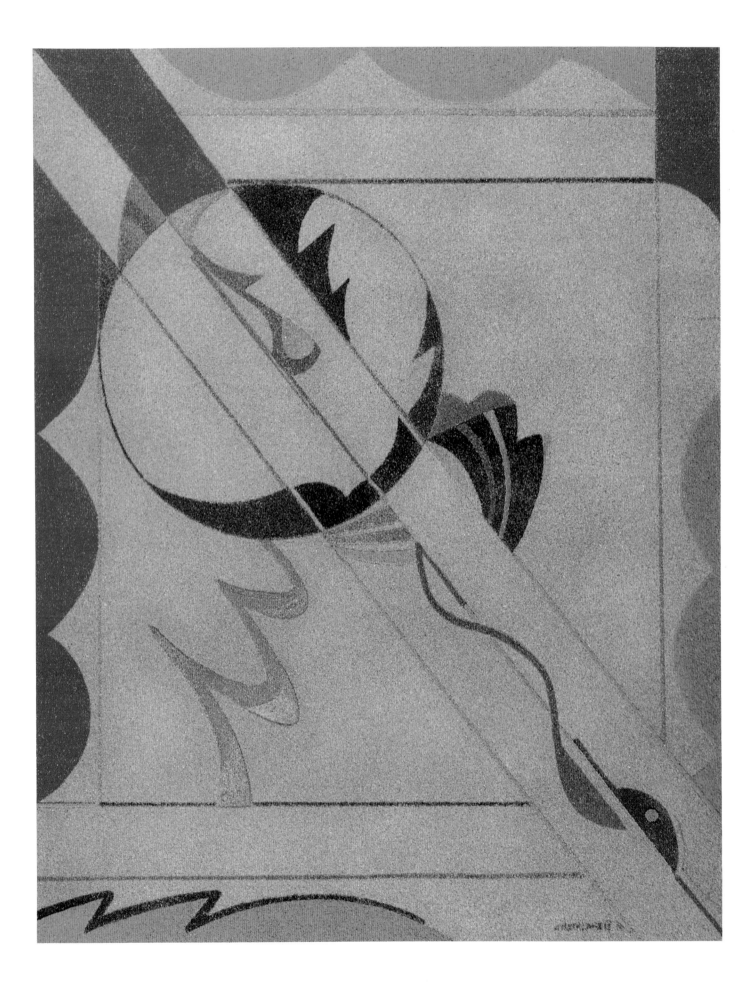

SACRED SERPENT'S WORLD

To the Hopi, the snake symbolizes closeness to the
earth, endurance, and influence on the clouds.
Many Indians of the Southwest believe that snakes
act as messengers to the underworld, carrying prayers
to the rain gods to bring the rain that nourishes the
Great Mother, the earth.

1976
20 x 16 inches
Sand on masonite
Plate 14

TEMPLE OF THE DAWN PEOPLE

"Dreams, visions, voyages into the deepest recesses of
the mind. The sound of drums, rasps, rattles, and
flutes. Endless hours chanting word-like sounds. Rituals,
rites of passage, celebrations of becoming. Dancing, heel
and toe, toe and heel, until the spirit of the deer invades
the emptiness within."

1981
40 x 30 inches
Acrylic and clay
on masonite
Plate 15

Shaman as Harlequin

We are the singers of silent songs,
The weavers of mystical dreams,
Dancers, stepping to the sound of skinless drums,
Shamans, whispering words unknown to man.

From the sun and stars we take the music for our songs,
From the wind, thread for our magic looms,
From water, the visions for our dreams,
And from the breasts of Mother Earth, the milk of life.

For the people, our dance is a dance of love.
For the sick, we weave blankets of well-being.
For the poor, our visions are of peace and plenty.
And for the sad, our songs are made of laughter.

Open your heart to the shaman song,
Dance with us the dance of love.
Sing with us the silent song, and know the joy of laugh-
*   ter.*
Weave with us a blanket to shield us from harm.

Open your mind to the shaman vision,
Share the peace and plenty that is all mankind's.
Shaman—together we will walk in beauty,
And find the beauty we seek within ourselves.

1983
14 x 11 inches
Acrylic on matboard
Plate 16

Shaman and Animal Spirits

"The shaman as warrior is you, with your ability
not just to heal from what you have experienced
but also to know that your experience is every
person's experience. This puts you in touch with
every man, every woman, every wounded animal,
every 'bent cloud.' Your shaking, your fevers, and
your fears put you in touch with the Earth. You don't
have to touch the Earth to know that it is shaking,
because it is shaking through you."

1982
10 x 8 inches
Acrylic on sand
on matboard
Plate 17

GREAT WATERS RISING

At the time of Great Waters Rising, the sacred Deer Spirit was confronted by the evil spirit from the Death Star. After ingesting the essence of peyote and datil,[12] the Deer Spirit confronted the evil spirit. Using the powers of clear vision and his own gifts, the Deer Spirit overcame his adversary, allowing the waters to recede and the earth to turn green and productive.

1981
16 x 12 inches
Acrylic on masonite
Plate 18

PEYOTE GUARDIANS

In the time of ancient dreaming, it happened that
the spirits of Grandfather and Grandmother merged
below the sacred red mountain. From their mixed
dreams sprang forth the Peyote Spirit. Another merging
brought forth the Black Beast (monster) and the Sky
Serpent to guard the Spirit of Peyote.

1981
20 x 16 inches
Acrylic on canvas
Plate 19

BARRIMUNDI GAP

Barrimundi Gap is an area in northern Australia that is sacred to the Aborigines. In 1979, lumber companies and mining intersests devastated part of the land. The Aborigines, fearing that it would be desecrated, protested to little avail until public interest began to have an effect. This painting was done as a shamanic prayer for the natives and the land.

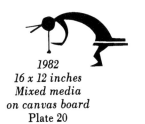

1982
16 x 12 inches
Mixed media
on canvas board
Plate 20

SKY GODS

The Butuloh came to Earth, visiting the people of
New Ireland in the South Pacific. They taught the
islanders how to navigate by holding out their hands
to feel the position of the stars, even in daylight, and
of the land masses that were out of sight, by sensing the
energies through the palms of their hands.

1970
20 x 12 inches
Acrylic on board
Plate 21

KAHDAM, KAHTI, AND BAHTI

The altarboard of African legend portrays the first man between his first companions, the Life-Giving Spirit and the Death-Granting Spirit. The giver of life is seen as irrational and illogical, symbolizing the nature of life itself. The giver of death walks on padded feet, quietly offering the gift of escape from the harsh reality of physical existence.

1982
22 x 30 inches
Acrylic and construction
on handmade paper
Plate 22

Guardians of the Four Corners

The artist-shaman, drawing upon his ability to contact the spirit world, attempts to determine the true nature of the spirit beings who are said to watch over the Four Corners area of the Navajo Reservation. He first encounters the Blue Guardian of the four directions (upper left). In a vision he then sees the Three-Horned Serpent guardian (upper right). Then he encounters the Twin Spirits of Good and Evil Nature, who are responsible for keeping the balance of nature (lower left). The last spirit he meets is the spirit of the Sacred Deer. This painting draws upon traditional native legends as well as my own way of seeing.

1982
30 x 24 inches
Acrylic on masonite
Plate 23

Guardians of the Underworld

A traditional Native American belief is that the underworld is the place where people who have died in this world continue to live. Unlike ideas of Hades or Hell, the underworld is similar to our own world, but without illness and distress. Guardians are placed at the opening to the underworld to frighten off any living beings who would attempt to enter this sacred land.

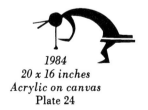

1984
20 x 16 inches
Acrylic on canvas
Plate 24

DREAM WORLD OF THE SHUWISH

The Shuwish, a tribe related to the Santa Barbara coastal California Indians, painted dream-world sequences in caves and on cliffs as far inland as the Colorado River. The figures represent "Shu-Shu," or the spirits of ancestors and spirit homes, the star-like figures. It was believed that such shamanic portrayals honored the ancient spirits and enlisted them in helping humankind.

As I was doing this painting, I sensed from the consciousness I was touching that many ancient traditions need to be brought back and included in ritual celebrations today. Ritual portrayal of the ancestors through shamanic art needs to continue so that we may remain aware of our interconnection with the ancestors and of our responsibility as participants in creation.

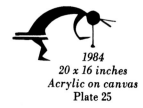

1984
20 x 16 inches
Acrylic on canvas
Plate 25

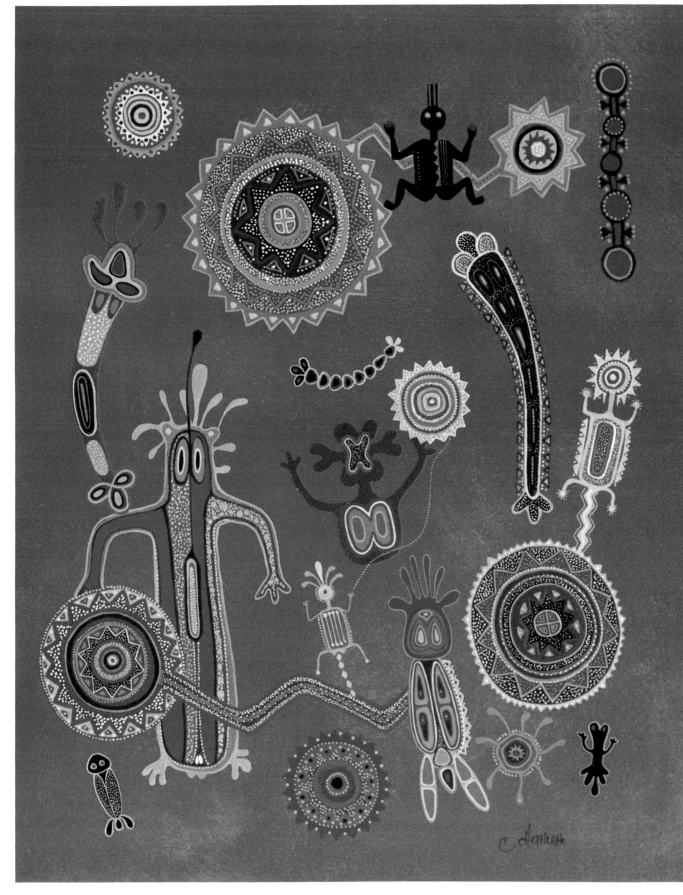

Fifth World Emergence

Some creation stories of the Southwest Indians trace
their evolution as a society by experiences in other
worlds or eras on this planet, preceding our present
time, the Fourth World. This image reflects the belief
that the transition to the Fifth World has already
begun. [LP]

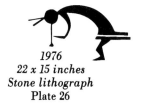

1976
22 x 15 inches
Stone lithograph
Plate 26

CONFLUENCE

. . . And a great blue star shall appear in the heavens. At that time, the twin worlds of Terran will pass through their spirit world and become one, as they were in the age of Atlan, united under the sign of the great serpent, Ka-an.

1982
24 x 19 inches
Mixed media
on handmade paper
Plate 27

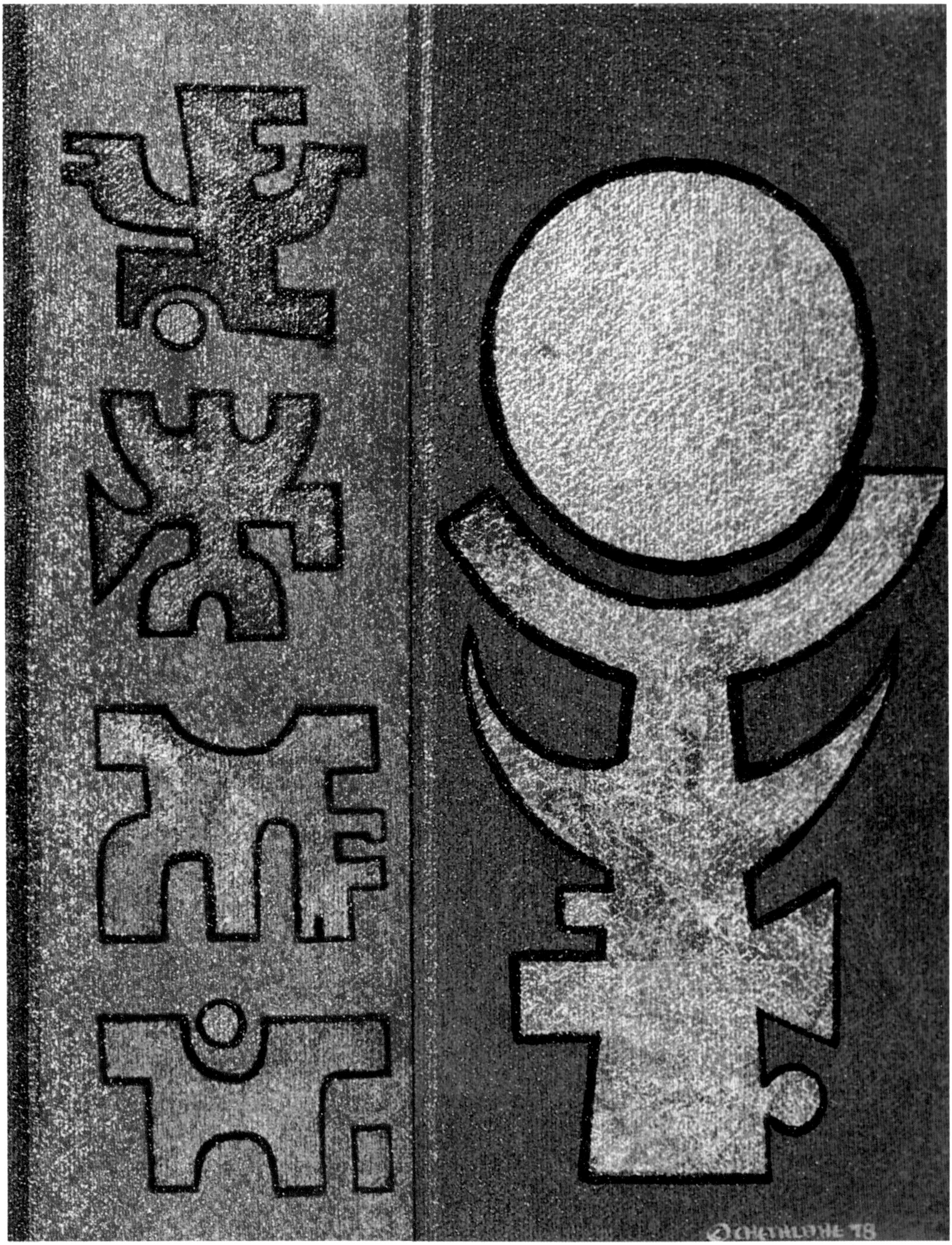

Page from Earth's History

The holder of these symbols is a high priest of the golden Orb whose secrets come from beyond the sun in the land of Katanar. YWH, holding the solar orb, bestows life (top left symbol) enriched threefold (three seasons of life, second symbol from top); bestows wisdom (third symbol from top); and holds the seed within the cradle of eternity (bottom symbol), to be born again.

1979
10 x 8 inches
Acrylic and gold leaf
on canvas
Plate 28

Axis Mundi

This painting is symbolic of life and death, multiplicity and unity, and the cosmic center that lies within everyone, the "world center" or axis which is everywhere at once.

The tree is springing from the female principle. On the right is the moon (female principle), and on the left is the sun (male principle). Below the tree is the flowering lotus from which rises a flame symbolizing the feminine energy. The flame to the right is female and to the left is male, representing the life forces. At the apex of the tree a winged crystal holds the combined male and female spirits. The crystals over the sun and moon represent transformation of male/female aspects into a united spirit. The calligraphy on the upper right is symbolic of unity, while the symbols on the left represent the multiplicity of reality as we experience it. Over the moon and sun are the male and female "sounds," and underneath the male and female circles are concealed the secret names of the male and female deities.

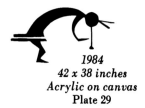

1984
42 x 38 inches
Acrylic on canvas
Plate 29

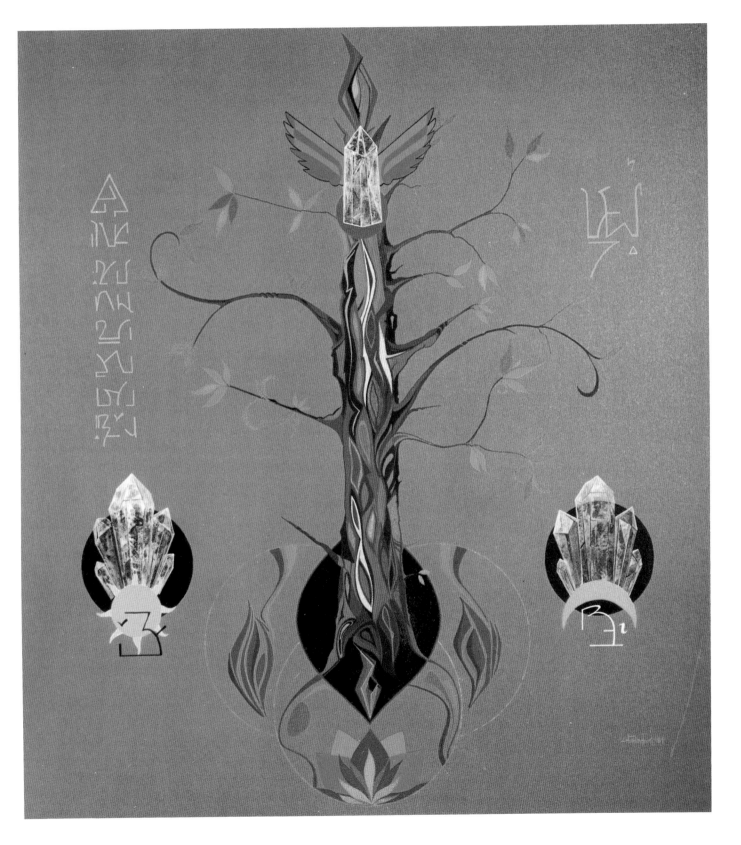

CRYSTAL FLAME

Deep within the galaxy where Sirius reigns lies a
crystal-laden asteroid. It is the mythic source of all
mathematical knowledge, the source of our dreams
and visions, the beacon that guides our fantasies.

1984
24 x 20 inches
Acrylic on masonite
Plate 30

Shifting Paradigm

All great truths are only myths that exist momentarily in the evolving greater consciousness. Like individuals, they die, to be reborn fresh and glorious in the minds of each new age. They may bear a resemblance to their forebears, but each brings with it new features of its own and seeks to find its place and meaning in the dancing dream that is the cosmos.

Now we need to move on to new myths. We are taking quantum leaps, and our paradigms are shifting rapidly.

The concepts we form and practice today create the foundation for the cultural and spiritual growth of the future. We need to achieve more than a simple desire to live in harmony with each other. If we are to survive, we must creatively respond to the spirit of transformation.

1982
24 x 19 inches
Acrylic and pencil
on handmade paper
Plate 31

NOTES

1. "Sonny..." In traditional Navajo speech, personal names tended to be avoided as a mark of respect for another's privacy and integrity. Direct eye contact was avoided for the same reason. [LP]

2. "From Bitter water I sprang..." refers to the Bitter Water Clan of the Navajo, Paladin's clan through the maternal line.

3. Wassily Kandinsky (1866-1944). Russian painter whose belief in a truth underlying all appearances gave rise to an art that was less abstraction *from* form than *to* form. Taught at the Bauhaus; with World War II, moved to Paris. Author of *Concerning the Spiritual in Art* (1917; original English title, *The Art of Spiritual Harmony*).

4. This experience was the seed for Paladin's healing. From this time on he began to work past his perceived physical limitations. In the late 1960s he stopped using his crutches and braces and learned to walk without their aid. [LP]

5. Marc Chagall (1887/89-1985). Russian Jewish artist especially beloved for his lyrical, poetic visions evoking the village life of his youth and rooted in a profound moral and religious sensibility. Much of his working life was spent in France.

6. Mark Tobey (1890-1976). American painter, resident in Europe from the mid-1960s on. A member of the Baha'i faith, whose belief in the oneness of humankind influenced his thought and work; also influenced by Eastern art and callig-

raphy. Developed a unique painting style, "white writing," characterized by dense linear patterning on darker grounds.

7. Morris Graves (1910–). American painter influenced by Mark Tobey and by Oriental mysticism; created dreamlike representational forms (notably his mysterious birds) and a highly expressive calligraphic brushstroke.

8. Pablo Picasso (1881–1973). Spanish painter, sculptor, and artistic innovator who broke through traditional boundaries of visual perception and expression to influence, directly or indirectly, the art-making of this century. Picasso, like Paladin, worked in different styles throughout his lifelong, prolific career. He was also deeply responsive to social injustice and oppression.

9. Dorothy Dunn's work with young Indian artists at the Santa Fe Indian School (founded in 1900) contributed to the development of early contemporary Indian fine arts. [LP]

10. The Sun Dance is a spiritual ceremony traditionally practiced by the Plains Indians of North America. Usually involving one or more days of communal prayer and offerings—including purification rituals (e.g., fasting, sweating), dance, and sound—the Sun Dance is performed for the renewal of the people and the earth.

11. These names were given to Paladin by his relatives at different times in his life to reflect his development as he matured.

12. Datil—jimson weed, a hallucinogenic herb.

Major Exhibitions, Collections, and Awards

Major Exhibits:

1966	Amon Carter Museum, Fort Worth
1967, 1975	Heard Museum, Phoenix
1969	William Penn Memorial Museum, Pittsburgh
1969–1972	National Indian Arts Exhibit, Scottsdale
1971–1982	Martin Gallery, Scottsdale
1972	Charles Bowers Memorial Museum, Santa Ana
1975, 1985	Albuquerque Museum, Albuquerque
1975	The Museum of Texas Tech University, Lubbock
1975	American Indian Art Center, New York
1980	Iowa State University, Ames
1981–1983	Cristof's, Santa Fe
1984	Navajo Tribal Museum, Window Rock, Arizona
1985	San Diego Museum of Man, San Diego
1985	Illuminarium Gallery, Larkspur, California
1988	Museum of Art, University of Arizona, Tucson

COLLECTIONS:

Albuquerque Museum, Albuquerque
Navajo Tribal Museum, Window Rock
Heard Museum, Phoenix
Minnesota Museum of Art
Carnegie Institute, Pittsburgh
Portland Art Museum, Portland
Detroit Institute of Fine Arts, Detroit
United States State Department, Washington, D.C.
United States Department of the Interior, Washington, D.C.
The White House, Washington, D.C.
United Nations, New York
Phoenix Civic Center Concert Hall, Phoenix

AWARDS AND HONORS:

1968	Carnegie Medal for Achievement in the Arts
1974	Distinguished Service in Education and the Arts, International Biographical Center, London, England
1976	Distinguished Achievement Award, International Biographical Center, London, England
1976–77	Community Leaders and Noteworthy Americans Award, American Biographical Institute

INDEX

*Lynda Paladin welcomes responses from readers
and inquiries from those interested in studying,
viewing, or purchasing David Paladin's art.
Original paintings and limited edition prints
are available through her.
She may be contacted by writing to:*

Painting the Dream
PO Box 11942
Albuquerque, NM 87192

*Please enclose a self-addressed, stamped envelope
if a reply is requested.*